First published in 2009. A catalogue record for this book is available from the British Library

ISBN 978-1-844257-08-9

Published by Haynes Publishing, Sparkford, Yeovil, Somerset BA22 7JJ, UK

Tel: 01963 442030 Fax: 01963 440001 Int. tel: +44 1963 442030 Int. fax: +44 1963 440001

E-mail: sales@haynes.co.uk Website: www.haynes.co.uk

Haynes North America Inc., 861 Lawrence Drive, Newbury Park, California 91320, USA

All images © Mirrorpix

Creative Director: Kevin Gardner

Packaged for Haynes by Green Umbrella Publishing

Printed and bound in Britain by J. H. Haynes & Co. Ltd.

Classic
SHIPS

Richard Havers

Thousands of years before any of our modern methods of transport were invented man travelled by boat. Later on, men travelling by ship proved that the world was round, discovering new lands and new continents. By the 20th century vast numbers of people used ships to emigrate to new lives in faraway lands; ships soon became floating palaces, representing the ultimate in sophistication. This book is a chronicle of our nautical heritage for the last hundred or so years and features everything from tall ships to small ships, working boats and lifeboats. In particular it is a salute to the liners that sailed the world's oceans carrying people to distant shores – port out, starboard home. This is a celebration of how man went down to the sea in ships.

"They that go down to the sea in ships, that do business in great waters."

The caption date for each picture is generally when the ship was built. However, in a few, obvious, instances it refers to a specific event that is recorded by the photograph.

TALL SHIPS

The term "tall ships" is a mid-20th century phenomena, brought into common usage with the advent of the Tall Ship Races; prior to that time ships with sails were an everyday sight with little of the glamour we attach to them today.

The windjammer was the workhorse of the rigged sailing ships, built to carry cargo around the world in the mid-19th to early 20th centuries. Constructed with iron or steel hulls, they could carry much more than their wooden counterparts, and with their three to five masts they could achieve average speeds as fast as 16 knots for a transatlantic crossing. Clipper ships were optimised for speed rather than an ability to carry large payloads; their name is derived from the fact that a fast horse was termed a "clipper". Barques are sailing ships with a particular pattern of sails that required fewer crew to handle them, while schooners are identified by their fore and aft masts.

Today tall ships are still being built, often as training ships for young people interested in a career at sea or for others who simply want to experience a sense of adventure. Modern rigged ships have the advantage of modern materials – particularly steel and aluminium – for use in their masts and rigging; this makes them lighter and much easier to handle.

For us today, used to the ever bigger and uglier ships for commercial and pleasure use, the sight of a fully rigged sailing ship is guaranteed to stir the imagination.

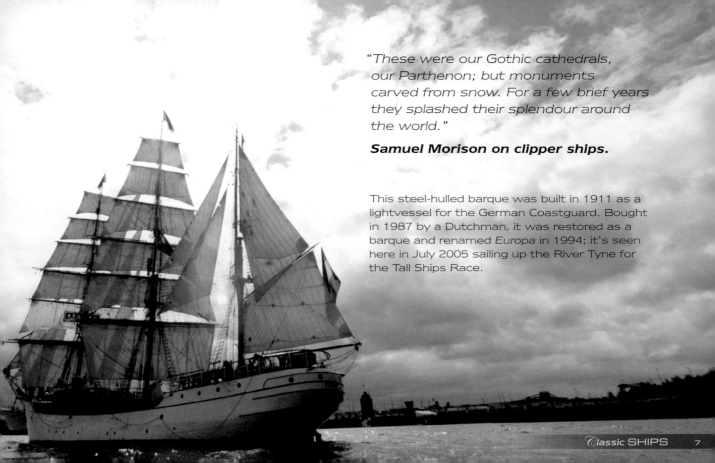

"*These were our Gothic cathedrals, our Parthenon; but monuments carved from snow. For a few brief years they splashed their splendour around the world.*"

Samuel Morison on clipper ships.

This steel-hulled barque was built in 1911 as a lightvessel for the German Coastguard. Bought in 1987 by a Dutchman, it was restored as a barque and renamed *Europa* in 1994; it's seen here in July 2005 sailing up the River Tyne for the Tall Ships Race.

In 1833 work began on the ship that would become the *Worcester*, though she was then called the *Royal Sovereign*. When she was eventually launched in 1860 she was named the *Royal Frederick*, and served as a war ship. But, with the advance of iron-sided ships she was already out of date and in 1876 was renamed the *Worcester* and turned into a training ship, in which capacity she continued to serve until 1939.

The *Cutty Sark* was the last clipper ship to be built as a merchant vessel, and after finishing her days as a training ship she was taken up the Thames on 15th December 1954 to a dry dock at Greenwich to become a museum. The larger photo was taken in March 1957 just before she was opened for the public.

Originally constructed in 1884 for the Dundee whaling fleet, the *Terra Nova* became an Arctic expedition support ship for the first time in 1894. This photo was taken at East India Dock in London in May 1910, a month before the ship set out on Captain Scott's ill-fated Antarctic expedition on 15th June 1910.

1
8
8
4

The *Herzogin Cecile* was built in 1902 as a merchant sailing ship for Norddeutscher Lloyd Bremen and was one of the fastest ships of her day. While bringing grain from Australia in the second fastest time ever in May 1936 she was grounded at Bolt Head, Devon, in thick fog; she was briefly refloated but broke up and sank at Kingsbridge Estuary near Salcombe.

The *Herzogin Cecile* at Belfast in 1934 (larger picture).

The windjammer *Penang* photographed sailing in the English Channel in 1935. She was originally the *Albert Rickmers*, built at Bremerhaven in 1905, but was taken over by Laeisz Line in 1910 and renamed the *Penang*.

The barque *Pamir* was a Flying P-Liner belonging to the German shipping company F Laisez and was the last commercial sailing ship to round Cape Horn in 1949. Two years earlier, in December 1947, she was photographed in the English Channel after a 13,000-mile journey from Wellington, New Zealand. She sank off the Azores in 1957 after being caught in a hurricane.

Launched in 1908 the 64 metre long schooner *Grossherzogin Elisabeth* is now a training ship. She's seen here competing in the 2005 Tall Ships Race.

Kruzenshtern was a Russian barque, built in Germany in 1926. She was another of the Flying P-Liners, the last in the line, and was originally called the *Padua*. In 1938-9 she sailed from Hamburg via Chile to Australia and back in 8 months and 23 days – an unbroken world record voyage for a tall ship. She was passed to Russia in 1946 as war reparation.

The *Artemis* was built in Norway as a whaling ship, operating mainly in the northern and southern polar seas until the 1940s. She was based in Oslo, fitted with a steam engine, two auxiliary masts and a variety of harpoon guns. In the 1950s she operated as a tramp freighter between Asia and South America, but by the end of the 1990s the *Artemis* was too small to operate as a competitive freighter. In 2001 she was converted into an elegant sailing ship.

ARTEMIS

In June 1953 the *Amerigo Vespucci*, an Italian sail training ship, visited Portsmouth, during celebrations for Queen Elizabeth II's coronation. Built in Naples and inspired by a 74-cannon ship of the line, she was originally designed to be a school ship, a role she is still performing.

The *Christian Radich* was built in Norway as a sailing training ship from a grant by a cavalry officer of the same name. She is a regular participant in tall ship events around the world; the photograph here is from July 1970.

Built for the Tall Ship's Youth Trust, the *Prince William* sails up the Tyne in 2005 as a participant in the Tall Ships Race.

WORKING SHIPS

If some working ships with sails have more than a hint of glamour, this is not true of other ships included here, which do little other than earn their keep. We have tried to bring you some of the more interesting working vessels and certainly some of those whose job it was to take people on holiday or on trips around the bay, and a little further, have gained a unique appeal with the passage of time.

There's also a tip of the hat to the River Clyde, Glasgow's river on which so many of the greatest ships ever to have been made were built. Glasgow's relationship with shipbuilding was for many years pivotal to its existence, with around 35,000 ships built there across two centuries. While there were great ships the majority were working ships, the unglamorous paddle steamers, tugs, ferries, tankers and tramp steamers.

At the end of this section is a small tribute to some of the hardest working ships of all – lifeboats. Founded in 1824 as the National Institution for the Preservation of Life from Shipwreck, the organisation became the Royal National Lifeboat Institute in 1854 – and continues to operate 230 lifeboat stations around Britain's coastline today, rescuing an average of over 20 people every day.

The Shell oil tanker *Megara* in October 1968 on her way up the River Thames to discharge her cargo of 206,000 tons of oil.

North Shields fish quay captured in 1880 when it had the largest privately owned trawler fleet in the country. Today it is one of the few commercial fishing ports remaining in northeast England.

The *Leopold II* built at the Scottish shipyard of Denny and Brothers at Dumbarton on the Clyde. On a measured mile the paddle steamer achieved a very fast 22.16 knots. In the First World War she became a troopship and is seen here arriving in Ostend carrying Belgian sailors from Le Havre in 1915; she was scrapped in 1922.

1893

These 19th century flat-bottomed barges were ideally suited to the Thames Estuary with its shallow waters. They were usually wooden, between 80 and 90ft long and carried almost every imaginable kind of cargo around the east coast of England. At the start of the 20th century there were over 2,000 of them. This photo dates from 24th September 1933, but after the Second World War the need for barges diminished as the transport of goods by road increased.

The *Roosevelt* was used by the Arctic explorer Robert Peary – "probably the most unpleasant man in the annals of polar exploration" – on his record-breaking expeditions in 1905-6 and 1908-9.

The Clyde paddle steamer *Eagle III* with its old-fashioned haystack boiler was built in 1910 and was operated by Buchanan's on their service from Glasgow to Rothesay. Photographed sailing down the River Clyde in 1930 she was run aground twice at Dunkirk when assisting with the embarkation of troops. She became an accommodation ship on Holy Loch before being scrapped in 1946.

1910

In November 1912, during the Balkans War, the *Daily Mirror* heard reports that five war correspondents were trapped in Silivri in Turkey. The newspaper chartered the tugboat *Alexandra* to mount a relief expedition, only to find that the correspondents had already left on another boat.

ALEXANDRA

This icebreaker was built in Newcastle-upon-Tyne in 1917. She was originally called *St Alexander Nevsky* but after the Russian Revolution was renamed the *Lenin*. Seen here in October 1948, she served throughout the war on convoy duties and finally retired in 1960 when a nuclear icebreaker named *Lenin* was launched.

23
22

Between 1929 and the outbreak of the
Second World War the Arctic survey vessel the
Discovery II carried out five commissions in the
Southern Ocean and a sixth in 1950-1, She is
seen here arriving at St Katharine's Docks in
London 11th May 1939.

The Wellington floating dock, built by Swan Hunter shipbuilders in Wallsend, seen here passing down the River Tyne, in the charge of tugs, on the first stage of its 13,500 mile voyage to New Zealand. When it was being moved in 1988 – its first move since arriving in New Zealand – it broke in two and sank.

A Yarmouth herring boat leaves the mouth of the River Yar in Norfolk for a fishing trip in the North Sea. By the time this photo was taken in 1935 the herring fishing industry, which had reached its peak at the start of the 20th century, was in relentless decline.

The 14,500 ton whaling ship, *Southern Venturer*, owned by Salvesen, was the first post-war whaler to be built in Britain.

When it was built at Swan Hunter's Neptune Yard on Tyneside in 1946 the *Monarch* was the largest cable ship in the world. She laid the first transatlantic telephone cable in 1955-6.

The *MV Princess Victoria* was one of the earliest roll-on, roll-off (RORO) ferries. Built in 1947 by Wm Denny & Bros, Dumbarton, she sank on 31st January 1953 in the North Channel with the loss of 133 lives; it was the worst maritime disaster involving a ferry until that involving *Herald of Free Enterprise* in 1987. British Railways used the *Princess Victoria* on the crossing from Stranraer in Scotland to Larne in Northern Ireland; she could accommodate 1,500 passengers and was the first purpose-built ferry of her kind to operate in British coastal waters.

By May 1951 when this photo was taken the Clyde shipbuilding industry in Glasgow was already in decline, having been the pre-eminent construction centre for all types of vessels from liners to warships. The *Queen Mary* had been built here in the 1930s and the *QE2* was still to be built; but after the heavy damage inflicted by Luftwaffe bombing during the Second World War the industry never fully recovered.

The Isle of Man Steam Packet Co steamer *Mona's Isle* operated year-round services from Douglas (Isle of Man) to Liverpool along with seasonal services from Douglas to Belfast, Dublin, Ardrossan, and excursions from Liverpool to Llandudno. The 2,490 ton ship, which could carry 2,393 passengers, is pictured having run aground after colliding with a fishing boat off Fleetwood.

The shifting sandbanks around the British coast make lightships the best way of alerting other ships to such dangers. The first lightship dates back to 1732. Shown here is the inappropriately named *Sunk*, Lightship One of the Trinity Lightships on the Goodwin Sands, photographed in May 1953.

Built in Denmark, the *Magga Dan* was one of a fleet of icebreaking cargo-passenger ships operated by J Lauritzen. She weighed almost 2,000 tons, could accommodate 36 passengers and was also fitted out with a hospital.

MAGGA DAN

This is the *Caroline*, the last lifeboat to be based at Blakeney, Norfolk. Crewed by 17 men, the *Caroline* was the most successful of all the Blakeney lifeboats but because of the silting up of Blakeney Harbour from around 1921 the lifeboat had to be moored in the harbour. By 1935 it was decided to dispense with a lifeboat at Blakeney Point, which makes this photograph from 30th March 1934 somewhat poignant.

1908

The *Peel* lifeboat is one of five on the Isle of Man. It was photographed being launched on 15th August 1913.

The Penlee Lifeboat Station was established in 1803. Photographed here is the *Severn Class Ivan Ellen*, seen leaving Newlyn dock in July 2006.

PLEASURE BOATS

A pleasure boat can be a craft used for messing about on a river or a lake, a sailing boat or even a gin palace. The pleasure boats featured here fit broadly into two categories: those that carry people off somewhere for pleasure, which of course includes liners and ferries but more typically boats that just do the short trips; and those that have given people more personal and individual pleasure, whether they be a king or queen, filmstar or just those who are rolling in it!

The *Lord of the Isles* was based at Inveraray. Her route was Greenock via Dunoon, Rothesay and the Kyles of Bute. Sold in 1909 to the Lochgoil and Inveraray Steamboat Company, she sailed to Lochgoilhead. After the First World War she went back to the Bute service before being scrapped at Port Glasgow in 1928, shortly after this photograph was taken.

Britannia was built on the Clyde for the Prince of Wales, later Edward VII, and after his death owned by George V. In 1921 George V refitted it out for racing, as shown here, as it passes Deal Pier. After George V's death in 1936, and in accordance with his wishes, it was towed out into the English Channel and sunk in deep water off the Isle of Wight.

The third Royal yacht to be named *Victoria and Albert*, she was built at Pembroke Dock; she was 4,700 tons and measured 380ft in length by 40ft in the beam. She was used regularly until the Second World War when she was laid up and used as an accommodation ship in Portsmouth harbour. In 1954 she was broken up at Faslane in Scotland.

The paddle steamer *Sempione* photographed at the village of Seelisberg, Switzerland, in 1936. She finally retired in 1961.

1903

Built in Leith, Scotland, in 1906 the *Kalizma*, a yacht belonging to Elizabeth Taylor, photographed moored off Tower Pier in London in August 1968. Richard Burton paid £80,000 in 1967 for the 165ft long boat as a present for Liz after she won an Oscar for *Who's Afraid of Virginia Woolf?* The yacht has recently been rebuilt and is based in Dubai.

The *Nahlin* was one of the last three large steam yachts built in Britain. She made her first appearance at Cowes Week in 1930, having been built for Lady Yule, a jute millionaire. Built by John Brown & Co Ltd of Glasgow, the yacht had a crew of 58 and was designed by G L Watson & Company. When this photo was taken in 1936 the *Nahlin* had been chartered by King Edward VIII; he and Mrs Wallace Simpson spent time together onboard.

Holidaymakers crammed onto the *Highlander* after a trip somewhere off the east coast of Britain in June 1930.

The steamer *Clanranald* at Glenfinnan Pier on Loch Shiel in the 1930s.

The *St Seiriol* leaving Liverpool
crowded with happy trippers on 10th
October 1949. She regularly sailed from
Liverpool to Llandudno and around Anglesey.
The *St Seiriol* was at Dunkirk in 1940 and tried to
assist the stricken paddler *Crested Eagle* when she
was destroyed. She finally retired in 1961.

ST SEIRIOL

The 83rd royal yacht, the *HMY Britannia*, is a 5,789 ton vessel with a crew of 19 officers and 217 ratings. Built at John Brown & Co Ltd on Clydebank, she undertook almost 1,000 visits with the Royal Family before she was decommissioned in 1997. She is now on permanent display at Edinburgh's Ocean Terminal.

Radio Caroline became the first European pirate radio station when it commenced broadcasting on Easter Sunday 1964 from the *MV Frederica*, a former passenger ferry.

LINERS

The two words 'ocean liner' conjure up all sorts of wonderful images in our minds – luxury, sophistication, port out, starboard home, faraway places, dressing for dinner, the captain's table and a lifestyle to which we would all probably like to become accustomed. What is easy to forget is that before the development of aircraft into large passenger jets the only way to travel vast distances in any kind of comfort was by sea. Even with the development of flying boat services in the 1930s the airlines still tipped their hats to the ocean liners . . . and it's still happening today. Why are pilots called 'captain'? More to the point, why are they even called pilots? The airline industry adopted just about everything possible from the ocean liners. Besides pilots and captains there are galleys, starboard and port wings, the cabin, the aircraft's hold, stewards, and the paperwork for each flight is referred to as the ship's papers. But as we all know, try as hard as they might, travel by air is a tedious business and nothing like the days of the luxury liners, except in perhaps one regard: economy class is often called steerage, which was the equivalent of third class on a liner.

By 1958 more than a million passengers made the trip across the Atlantic by air – the date was a landmark, the first year that aircraft carried more passengers across the Atlantic than the liners – something that was considered a preposterous idea only a decade earlier when BOAC predicted that they might carry around 40,000 travellers a year. Today this number is exceeded on a daily basis on flights between the UK and the United States, while taking the boat from Southampton to New York only happens as part of a cruise.

While the transatlantic route was the busiest for boat travel, as it is for air travel today, the demands of Britain's far-flung empire, and to a lesser extent those of other nations, encouraged the development of bigger, faster and more comfortable boats. But behind the practicalities of travel lay the competitiveness between nations and shipping lines to have the biggest, the fastest and the most comfortable boats – not so much for commercial reasons as for the pride that went with it.

The Blue Riband awarded for the fastest Atlantic crossing is a manifestation of the national and corporate rivalry that then existed. The award was created by shipping companies in the 1860s:

individual blue pennants were flown from the ship's mast in recognition of the award for the eastbound and westbound crossings. Many of the liners featured in this book have held the coveted award, including the *Lusitania*, *Mauretania*, *Bremen*, *Normandie*, *Queen Mary* and *United States*.

Today liners are in fact cruise ships, and the last of the great liners, the *Queen Elizabeth II* or *QE2*, retired in 2008 to become a floating hotel in Dubai. It is for some a tragic end for a once great ship and the lineage of liners that it represents, but for others there is still the opportunity to spend a night aboard one of the great transport icons.

The *SS President Roosevelt* in February 1926.

The 31,550 ton Cunard liner *Lusitania* took less than 20 minutes to sink after she was torpedoed on 7th May 1915 off the Old Head of Kinsale, Ireland. Some 1,198 people were killed as a result of the sinking, which played a significant part in turning world opinion against Germany. On her first transatlantic crossing she secured the Blue Riband, which was formerly held by the German ship *Deutschland*.

Built by Swan, Hunter and Wigham Richardson at Wallsend, the super liner *Mauretania* was the largest and fastest liner to have been built at the time. Her revolutionary steam turbines propelled the 31,938 ton liner at 24 knots carrying 2,165 passengers and over 800 crew. She is seen here leaving the River Tyne for her first trials at sea on 7th April 1907; the *Mauretania* stayed in service with Cunard until 1934.

1906

Originally called the *Kaiserin Auguste Victoria*, this ship was built in Stettin for the Hamburg America Line. The 24,581 ton liner was handed over to the Allies as war reparation, and after briefly sailing under a Cunard flag she became the *Empress of Scotland*, sailing regularly between Quebec and Europe for Canadian Pacific. In 1930 when the *Empress of Britain* was launched this grand old lady was sold for scrap, catching fire in the breakers dock in Blyth in Northumberland on 11th December 1930.

Classic SHIPS

The *RMS Olympic*, sister ship to the *Titanic*, is seen here arriving at Southampton docks. The *RMS Olympic* was the first of the three sisters to be completed and was launched in 1911. She also completed service in the First World War and later returned to carry passengers in great luxury. Of the three sisters, *RMS Olympic* was the only one to complete a full, serviceable life. She completed her last journey in 1935 and was later scrapped at Palmers Shipyard, Jarrow.

1912

Originally named the *Imperator* and built in Hamburg, the 52,226 ton ship spent the First World War in the port of Hamburg, having made her maiden transatlantic crossing in June 1913. After the war she was handed over to Great Britain and bought by Cunard in 1921; they renamed her the *Berengaria*. This most popular liner caught fire in New York in March 1938. She was sold for scrap and was photographed entering the River Tyne on 9th December 1938. Work began to break her up but was interrupted by the Second World War, so it was only in 1946 that the hull was finally towed to Rosyth to complete the task.

The Daily Mirror

THE MORNING JOURNAL WITH THE SECOND LARGEST NET SALE.

No. 2,645.   TUESDAY, APRIL 16, 1912   One Halfpenny.

DISASTER TO THE TITANIC: WORLD'S LARGEST SHIP COLLIDES WITH AN ICEBERG IN THE ATLANTIC DURING HER MAIDEN VOYAGE.

The most famous liner of all time – due in no small part to the film of the same name – the *Titanic* was known around the world for the saddest of reasons. Launched in May 1911 and making her maiden voyage on 10th April 1912, she sank four days later after hitting an iceberg; 2 hours and 40 minutes was all it took for the 46,328 ton liner to sink.

Built in Belfast at Harland & Wolff, the vessel belonged to the White Star Line and was at the time the largest liner in the world. It was capable of carrying 3,547 people, including crew, but on this first trip from Southampton to New York there were 2,222 passengers and crew on board. Some 1,517 people died, though over 60 per cent of first-class passengers survived; the majority of those killed died from hypothermia. All the children in first and second class survived and almost all the women from first class and 86 per cent from second class. Three-quarters of all the third-class passengers were lost.

Perhaps most telling of all was the number of crew families who suffered loss: 1,000 families in Southampton alone were directly affected. Almost every street in the Chapel district of the town lost more than one resident and over 500 households lost a member.

Titanic and *SS New York* – two funnels almost in collision, 10th April 1912.

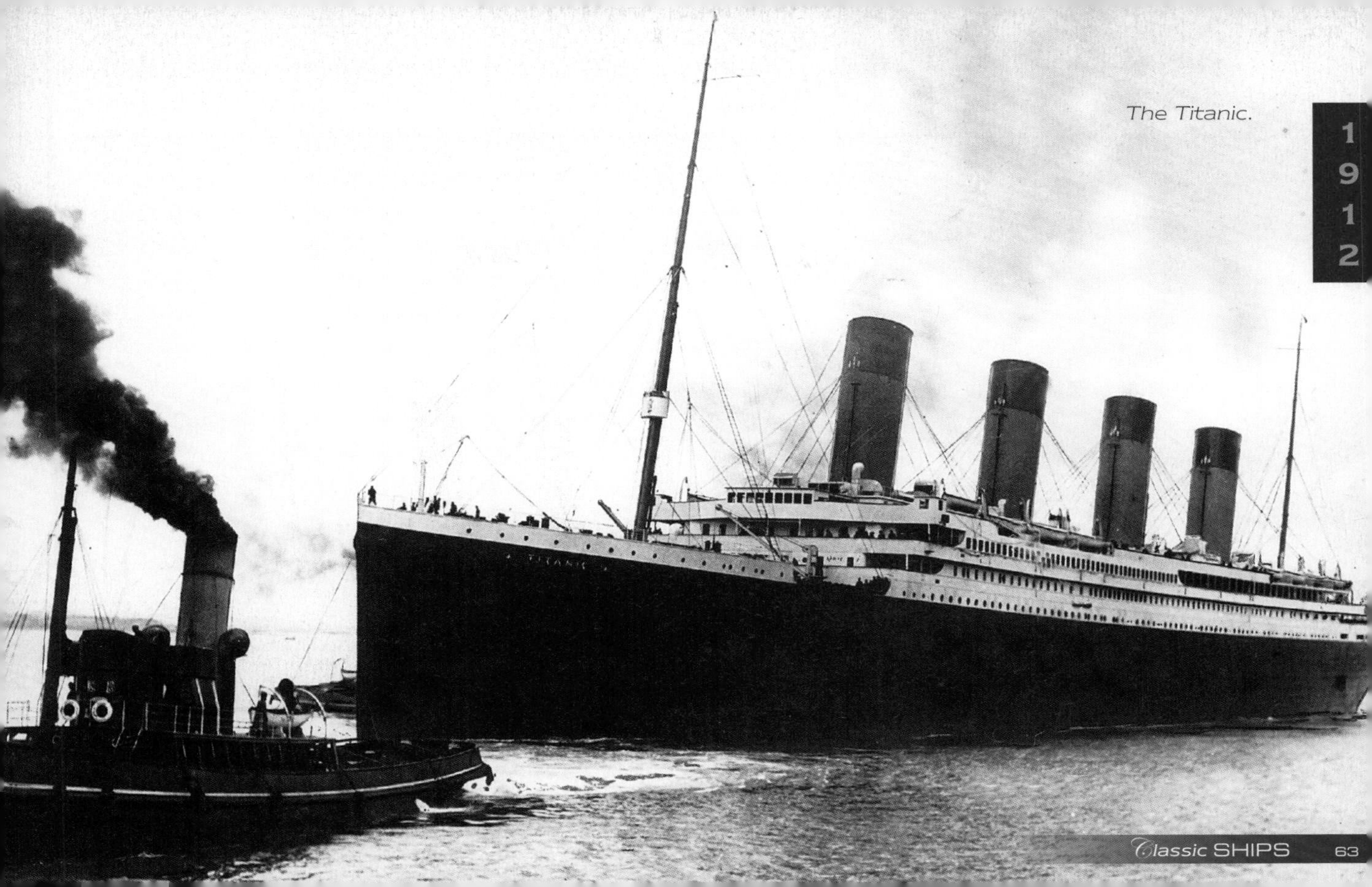

The Titanic.

1912

The second-class promenade deck of the *Titanic*.

Originally called the *Columbus*, this ship belonged to Norddeutscher Lloyd, though the 35,000 ton liner was handed over to the White Star Liner in 1920 as part of Germany's war reparations. Renamed the *Homeric*, she had a larger proportion of her accommodation allocated to steerage class, harking back to a time when there were many immigrants crossing the Atlantic. Following a short career as a cruise ship her days ended shortly after Cunard took over the White Star Line in 1934. The photo was taken at Southampton docks before she departed for New York in April 1932.

The originally named *SS Vaterland* briefly crossed the Atlantic for the Haphag Line in 1914. When war broke out she was docked in New York, where she was seized by the US Navy. In 1917 the 54,282 ton liner was renamed *The Leviathan* and worked as a troopship. After the First World War she was refurbished, and from 1923 worked for United States lines on transatlantic crossings. Pictured on 12th September 1924 she continued in service until 1934, finally being broken up in 1938.

The *RMS Aquitania* was built for Cunard by John Brown & Co Ltd at Clydebank and sailed to New York in her maiden voyage in May 1914. Pictured here on 15th May 1921 the 45,647 ton liner survived service in two world wars and finally retired in 1949, having carried over 1.2 million passengers.

The French Line's *Paris* was laid down in 1913, launched in 1916 but not completed until 1921 because of the war. On her completion she was the largest French liner, at 34,569 tons. Seen here at anchor in 1933 she caught fire in April 1939 while docked at Le Havre and sank; she stayed there until after the war ended.

Photographed in February 1935 the 22,517 ton liner the *Empress of Canada* was built for Canadian Pacific by Fairfield Shipbuilding at Govan on the River Clyde. Based in Vancouver, she regularly sailed to Japan and Hong Kong and remained in service until the outbreak of the Second World War, when she was converted to a troopship. She was torpedoed and sank in March 1943 with the loss of almost 400 lives out of the 1,800 people on board.

Built in Hamburg and originally named the *Bismarck*, this 56,551 ton ship was the largest liner in the world at the time of her completion in 1922. Handed over to Britain after the war she was renamed the *Majestic* by her new owners, the White Star Line. She is seen here shortly before her maiden voyage to New York in April 1922. In 1936 she made her last voyage and was bought by the British government for conversion to a training ship, *HMS Caledonia*. Based in Rosyth on the Firth of Forth, the war interrupted her career and she caught fire and burnt out at Rosyth in September 1939.

The *Athenia* has the dubious honour of being the first ship sunk by Germany in the Second World War. Built by Fairfield Shipbuilding at Govan, the 13,465 ton ship belonged to Anchor Donaldson Ltd and was used on the company's routes to Canada. On 3rd September 1939, just hours after war was declared, she was sunk by a U-boat: 118 passengers and crew were lost including 28 of the 300 Americans on board. Hitler ordered all evidence of the incident to be suppressed, and so the U-boat's log was rewritten.

Built in Cammell, Laird & Co Birkenhead for the French company CGT the 17,738 ton liner *De Grasse* operated from Le Havre to New York until 1940 when the Germans seized her. Sunk in 1944 she was raised and refitted and reentered service in 1945 having had her funnels reduced from two to one. She was bought by Canadian Pacific in 1953, painted white and renamed the *Empress of Australia* before being sold to an Italian company who called her the *Venezuela*; she was lost off Cannes in 1962.

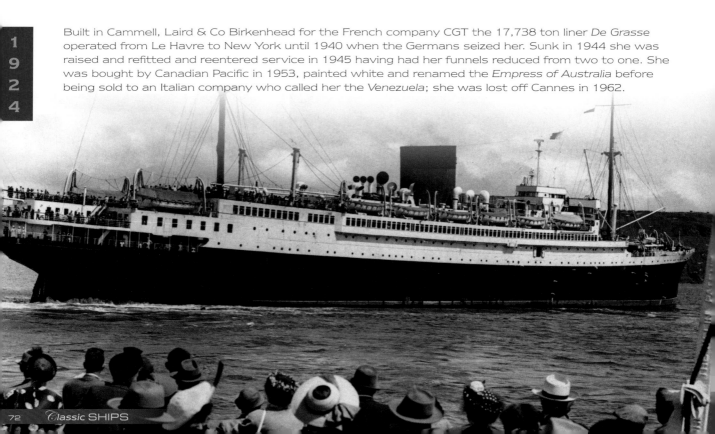

The *Princess Marguerite* was built by John Brown & Co Ltd at Clydebank in 1925 for Canadian Pacific Steamships Ltd in Montreal; she is seen here leaving Clydebank for the first time. In 1939 she was requisitioned by the Ministry of War and used as a troopship. She was lost in August 1942 after being torpedoed by a U-boat in the Mediterranean; despite the loss of 49 lives over 1,000 soldiers and crew were saved.

The *Asturias* was built by Harland & Wolff, Belfast, for Royal Mail meat transports; in 1939 her forward funnel was removed. She saw service as an emigrant ship to Australia making over 20 voyages carrying around 1,200 passengers on each sailing; she is photographed here in February 1950 leaving Southampton for Melbourne and Sydney. Sold for scrap in 1957 she was used in the film *A Night to Remember* to depict the *Titanic* in the lifeboat-lowering scenes.

The 9,356 ton *Ascania* was originally named the *Florida* when she was built in France. Sunk in a German air attack in 1942 she was refloated and repaired, having gone from being a two-funnel to a one-funnel vessel. Renamed the *Ascania* in 1955, she made a number of transatlantic voyages before eventually becoming a cruise ship in 1966 and then scrapped two years later.

The 21,239 ton Greek cruise liner the *Queen Frederica* is seen here laid up on the River Dart in May 1972. Designed by William Francis Gibbs, who became the most famous American ship designer of the 20th century, she was christened *Malolo* for service on the Matson Line San Francisco to Honolulu route. Later renamed the *Matsonia* she was later still named the *Atlantic* before becoming the *Queen Frederica* in 1954; she finally retired in 1977, after 50 years' service.

The *Bremen*, built for the Norddeutsche Lloyd Line, was a 51,656 ton ship that could cruise at 27.5 knots. She first sailed for New York in July 1929 from Bremerhaven and made the last peacetime crossings of the Atlantic by any ship in September 1939. Photographed here leaving Southampton on 13th December 1936 she was set alight while in Bremerhaven by a crew member with a grudge against the company; she was gutted and finally broken up in 1946.

The New Zealand Line ship *Rangitata*, photographed at London's Royal Albert Docks in January 1957. The 16,737 ton ship regularly sailed to New Zealand via the Panama Canal in 32 days. Having worked as a troopship in the Second World War she was sold for scrap in 1962, along with her sister ship the *Rangitiki*.

Originally named the *Duchess of Richmond* and built by John Brown & Co Ltd for Canadian Pacific on the Clyde, this 20,022 ton liner was renamed the *Empress of Canada* in 1947 following the loss of the original ship of that name. Seen here in August 1948, she caught fire and capsized in Liverpool docks in January 1953 and was scrapped later in the year.

The French Liner *L'Atlantique* was the most luxurious ship on the Compagnie de Navigation Sud Atlantique's routes from Europe to South America. The 42,000 ton liner could carry 1,238 passengers and a crew of 663, but caught fire on 5th January 1933 on her way to Le Havre for a refit, after making only nine round trips to South America; nine crew died while fighting the fire that destroyed her interiors. After protracted legal battles between the insurers and the owners she was eventually scrapped in 1936.

Built in Hamburg by Blohm and Voss, the *Monte Rosa*, as she was originally called, was used principally for cruising. Captured as a prize of war she became the *Empire Windrush* and was used as a troopship; it is in this role that she was photographed in June 1947 in the Thames en route for the Middle East. She later undertook emigrant sailings to Australia as well as bringing Jamaicans to Britain before she burned out in 1954 on a trooping voyage.

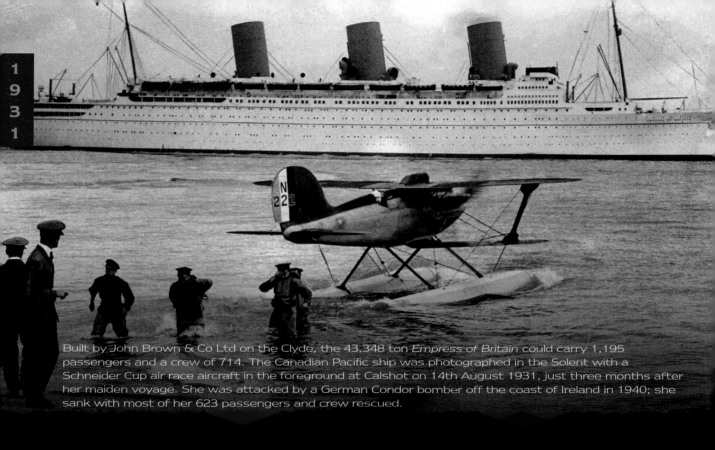

1931

Built by John Brown & Co Ltd on the Clyde, the 43,348 ton *Empress of Britain* could carry 1,195 passengers and a crew of 714. The Canadian Pacific ship was photographed in the Solent with a Schneider Cup air race aircraft in the foreground at Calshot on 14th August 1931, just three months after her maiden voyage. She was attacked by a German Condor bomber off the coast of Ireland in 1940; she sank with most of her 623 passengers and crew rescued.

The Furness Bermuda Line operated from New York to Bermuda with this ship, the *Monarch of Bermuda*, and her sister ship the *Queen of Bermuda*. Seen here on the River Tyne on 17th August 1931 where she was built, the 22,234 ton ship could carry 800 passengers. She remained on the New York route until war came and she was converted to a troopship. Shortly after the war ended she was gutted by fire but was rebuilt as an emigrant ship, the *New Australia*, before becoming the *Arkadia* in 1958; she was finally

The *Georgic*, built at Harland & Wolff in Belfast, was the last ship to be constructed for the White Star Line before its merger with Cunard. Her maiden voyage was in June 1932 from Liverpool to New York, before she took over the Southampton-New York route a year later. The 27,739 ton liner was converted to a troopship before being sunk in the Gulf of Suez in 1941. Despite being almost completely burnt out it was decided to rebuild her, a task completed in 1944 – although in the process she lost a funnel. Seen here on the River Tyne in December 1948, she remained with Cunard until 1954; she was scrapped in 1956 after briefly working as an Australian troopship.

The *Normandie* was originally built as a 79,280 ton liner but, in order to remain the largest passenger ship in the world, she was increased in size to 83,423 tons when the *Queen Mary* was built. She carried 1,972 passengers and a crew of 1,345. Seen here leaving Le Havre for Southampton and New York on 29th May 1935, the *Normandie* remained in service until war broke out, when she was in New York, which is where she remained until the Fall of France in 1940; she was then seized for use as a troopship. During her refit she caught fire, partially sank and all work on her ceased until she was scrapped in 1946.

1934

Originally built at a cost of £3.5 million for the Cunard White Star Line, the 81,237 ton *Queen Mary* sailed the Atlantic for over 30 years. Work began on building her in 1930, on the Clyde, and she was launched four years later, entering service less than two years later. Able to accommodate 2,139 passengers – 776 in first class, 784 in tourist class and 579 in third class – she had a crew of 1,100. There is strong evidence to suggest that she was originally to be called the *Queen Victoria*, but when the chairman of Cunard asked King George V's permission to "name the liner after Britain's greatest ever Queen", the king replied, "His wife would be delighted." There was some criticism of the *Queen Mary*'s design as a liner, especially her restrained art deco interiors when compared with her main rival, the French ship *Normandie*. The two ships vied for the Blue Riband, which they both held for various periods until 1938 when the *Queen Mary* regained it, in both directions, with an average speed of 30.99 knots westbound and 31.69 knots eastbound; the record stood until 1952 when the *United States* captured it. During the Second World War she served as a troopship, after the war was over she was refitted for passenger work and continued her role as Britain's transatlantic flagship, along with her sister ship the *Queen Elizabeth*. She was sold to a company in Long Beach, California, where she became a tourist attraction – a role she still performs today, in addition to having become a hotel and museum.

The *Queen Mary* passes under New York Bridge in October 1964.

The *Queen Mary* was launched at John Brown's shipyard in Clydebank, on 26th September 1934.

The *Queen Mary* makes her way down the River Clyde to commence her sea trials.

The *Queen Mary* starts her maiden voyage on 27th May 1936.

The *Queen Mary* passes through the Solent for the last time as she sails to her retirement in Long Beach, California, in November 1967.

The Orient Line ship the *Orion* was the first British liner to be fitted with air conditioning in all rooms. Built by Vickers-Armstrong in Barrow-in-Furness, Cumbria, she could carry 1,110 passengers and 466 crew and sailed for Australia on her maiden voyage in September 1935. After serving as a troopship she was back to her civilian duties in 1947 having had a refit to accommodate 1,250 passengers. Photographed here heading down the River Thames on 6th May 1949, she remained in service until 1963, when she was scrapped.

Named after a 16th century King of Poland, the liner *Batory* was a 14,287 ton ship that served with distinction as a troopship during the war before returning to civilian duties in 1946. She remained in service until 1971, when she was scrapped. Photographed here on 5th January 1954.

The second ship to be named the *Mauretania* is photographed at the Prince's landing stage, Liverpool, on 24th April 1947. The 35,738 ton liner, built by Cammell Laird in Birkenhead, was owned by Cunard White Star Line and could carry 1,360 passengers, although this was later reduced to 1,127 in 1962. By 1965, with the change in the economic fortunes of the big liners, she was scrapped.

The 27,000 ton motor liner *Dominion Monarch* was the largest ship operating regularly from Britain to Australia and New Zealand when she made her maiden voyage in February 1939. She worked as a troopship during the war and in 1948 was returned to her owners, Shaw Savill, for use on their Australasian routes. She was photographed entering the River Tyne for an extensive refit in 1953; she was scrapped in 1962.

The 25,600 ton *Andes* was built at Harland & Wolff and failed to make her maiden voyage before war broke out, when she was converted to a troopship. She had a post-war refit in 1947 and began working as a 500-passenger liner to South America – Rio de Janeiro, Santos, Montevideo and finally Buenos Aires. By the 1960s she became a cruise ship and is seen here docking at Southampton in December 1970.

THE QUEEN ELIZABETH

1
9
3
4

Laid down at John Brown & Co Ltd on the Clyde in December 1936 and launched on 27th September 1938, she made her maiden voyage on 3rd March 1940. At 83,672 tons she was the largest liner ever to have been built, a record that was to last for another 56 years. She could carry 2,283 passengers and had a crew of over 1,000. Her maiden voyage was to New York, although the original destination was Southampton – fortunately this was changed at the very last minute, and the night when she should have been in dock at Southampton the port was bombed by the Luftwaffe. In New York she joined the *Queen Mary* and the *Normandie*, the only occasion the world's three greatest liners were in port together. After serving as a troop transport during the war she started serving New York on Cunard's twice weekly service. In the 1960s she also began cruising, but this was a role to which she was not well suited as her deep draft prevented her entering a number of ports. The *Queen Elizabeth*, along with the *Queen Mary*, was retired in 1969 and sold to a company for display in Florida alongside her sister ship in Long Beach. The plan failed for various reasons and she was then sold to a Hong Kong businessman who wanted to use her as a university at sea. During a refit she caught fire and sank in Hong Kong harbour on 9th January 1972.

The *Queen Elizabeth* leaves Southampton for the last time on 29th November 1968.

The *Queen Elizabeth* leaving Southampton in 1948.

1934

The *Queen Elizabeth* moored alongside Southampton's Western dock before her final departure to New York on 29th November 1968.

85

Originally launched as the *Willem Ruys* for the Royal Rotterdam Line, she made her maiden voyage in December 1947; the 21,119 ton ship could accommodate 900 passengers. Sold to an Italian cruise line she became the *Achille Lauro*. Photographed here at Southampton in 1975, some 10 years later she became world famous when she was hijacked by the PLO in the Mediterranean.

The 34,183 ton *Caronia* photographed on her speed trials off the coast of Arran on 18th December 1948. Nicknamed the 'Green Goddess' on account of the pale green colour scheme on her hull, she was built as a duel purpose liner-cruise ship and could accommodate 932 passengers. She made her first world cruise in 1951 and her final Southampton-New York crossing at the end of 1967. After being sold and renamed the *Caribia* she made just two cruises before an explosion in her engine room; she ended her days in a Pacific harbour in 1974 en route to Taiwan, where she had been sold as scrap.

The 15,902 ton *Gothic* was built by Swan Hunter & Wigham Richardson on the River Tyne. She made her maiden voyage from Liverpool to Sydney in December 1948 and on 12th January 1952, after a major refit, she sailed for Mombasa with Princess Elizabeth and the Duke of Edinburgh on board as part of a royal tour. In 1953 she was again used as a royal ship for a trip by the now Queen Elizabeth to Australia and New Zealand. In 1968 on a voyage from New Zealand to the UK her bridge caught fire; she was subsequently sold for scrap.

The *Patricia*, photographed here leaving the River Tyne for the first time, was another liner built by Swan Hunter & Wigham Richardson. Belonging to Swedish Lloyd, she operated between Gothenburg and London's Tilbury docks during the summer and cruised in the Caribbean in the winter. She was renamed the *Adriane* in 1957, the first of many renamings, and finally retired as the *Empress 65* in 1997.

The *United States* arriving at Southampton after making a record-breaking maiden voyage on 8th July 1952, capturing the Blue Riband from the *Queen Mary*. The ship lost this eastbound record in 1990 but still holds the westbound record. The 53,330 ton ship carried 1,928 passengers, a crew of 900 and had a top speed of 38.3 knots. She was taken out of service in 1969 and after a whole series of schemes was suggested she is today moored in Philadelphia awaiting the next scheme by which she might once again sail the seas.

The 17,029 ton Union Castle Liner *Braemar Castle* was built in Belfast by Harland & Wolff. She could carry 453 passengers and was built for the round Africa run, out via Suez and back via the Atlantic or vice versa. She was scrapped at Faslane in 1966.

The *Kungsholm* was built in the Netherlands for the Swedish American Line as a combined liner-cruise ship. The 21,164 ton ship could carry 802 passengers with a crew of 418. In 1965 she was sold to Germany and renamed the *Europa*; later still she was renamed the *Columbus C*, but sank in Cadiz harbour in 1984 after ramming a breakwater.

The 13,360 ton *City of York* photographed on her maiden voyage to Beira in November 1953. Belonging to the Ellerman & Bucknall Line she was the last of their ships to sail from Cape Town in 1971. Sold to a Greek company, she was renamed *Mediterranean Sky* in 1971 and was finally abandoned in 2002, having been grounded in shallow water.

CITY OF YORK

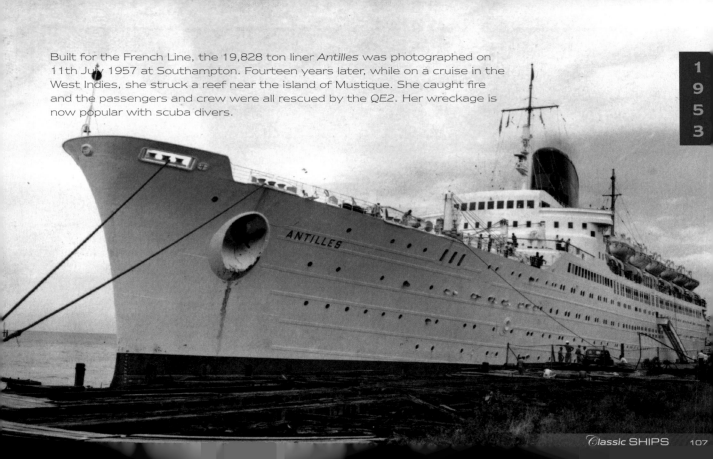

Built for the French Line, the 19,828 ton liner *Antilles* was photographed on 11th July 1957 at Southampton. Fourteen years later, while on a cruise in the West Indies, she struck a reef near the island of Mustique. She caught fire and the passengers and crew were all rescued by the *QE2*. Her wreckage is now popular with scuba divers.

1953

The 21,637 ton *Ivernia* of Cunard photographed leaving John Brown's Yard at Clydebank to begin trials off the Isles of Arran in 1955. The *Ivernia* was the sister ship to *Sylvania*, *Saxonia* and *Carinthia*, and sailed regularly on Cunard's Canadian routes. In 1963 the *Ivernia* was rebuilt as a cruise ship and renamed *Franconia*; 10 years later she was sold to a Russian company as the *Feodor Shalyapin*; she was scrapped in 2004.

The *Carinthia* pictured leaving John Brown's Yard at Clydebank before making her maiden voyage on to Montreal in June 1956. Sold to Sitmar Lines in 1968 as a cruise ship, she was renamed the *Fairland*. After further sales and several more name changes she ended her days as a casino cruise ship before being scrapped in 2001.

The 18,700 ton *Bergensfjord* was built by Swan, Hunter & Wigham Richardson on the Tyne for the Norwegian America Line; here she is photographed leaving the river on 29th May 1956. In 1971 she was bought for the French Line and became the second liner to be called the *De Grasse*, as a replacement for the *Antilles*. Sold two years later she became the *Rasa Sayang*. She caught fire in 1980 and later sank.

In June 1955, some 50 years after the first ship of this name had been launched, the new *Empress of Britain* was under construction at Fairfield's Shipyard at Govan on the River Clyde. The 25,516 ton vessel made over 120 transatlantic crossings for Canadian Pacific before she was sold to a Greek company and renamed the *Queen Anna* in 1964. After being sold on a number of times more she finally retired in 2008.

1957

The *Empress of England* photographed making her way up the River Tyne on 15th March 1957. She made her maiden sailing from Liverpool to Montreal a month later for Canadian Pacific. Sold in 1970 to Shaw, Savill & Albion, she was renamed *Ocean Monarch* and became a full-time cruise ship; it was a career that lasted only two years, since she was withdrawn from service in the summer of 1975.

The P&O Liner *Oriana* was built at Vickers-Armstrong in Barrow-in-Furness and served Australia from Southampton. She was repainted white, having previously been corn coloured, and by 1970 when this photograph was taken she was spending the majority of her time cruising. The 41,915 ton ship could accommodate 1,677 cruise passengers. Sold by P&O in 1981, by the 1990s she was used in China as a theme park until in 2004 she began listing to port after a gale and was scrapped a year later.

The *Empress of Canada* seen here being towed to the quayside on the River Mersey at the start of her maiden voyage on 24th April 1961 from Liverpool to Montreal. The 27,284 ton liner could carry 1,048 passengers and regularly plied the Atlantic until she was sold to Carnival Cruise Lines in 1972; they renamed her *Mardi Gras*. After numerous sales and renamings she ended her days as the *Apollo* in 2003.

The P&O cruise ship *Canberra* returns to Southampton Water on 13th July 1982 after service as a troopship during the Falklands War. She started as a 45,270 ton ship able to accommodate 2,238 passengers, a number which by 1973 was reduced to 1,737. She remained in service until 1997, when she was scrapped.

1962

The French Line's 66,343-liner *France* regularly crossed the Atlantic and did winter cruising before she was sold in 1974, when this photograph was taken: by this time she had made 377 crossings and 93 cruises. She was then mothballed and, in 1979, sold to Norwegian Cruise Lines and renamed *Norway*. In 2003 she was damaged by a boiler explosion and finally scrapped in 2008 following protracted issues over where this operation should be done given the large amount of asbestos used in her construction.

The Russian Liner *Ivan Franko* seen arriving at London's Tilbury docks on 6th December 1964, shortly after her maiden voyage. Built in Wismar, East Germany, she served the Black Sea Shipping Company until she was scrapped in 1997.

The 20,995 ton double hulled cruise ship the *Radisson Diamond* was photographed on 26th May 1992, shortly after her maiden voyage. Since 2005 she has operated as the *Asia Star*, a casino cruise ship.

The 76,152 ton cruise ship *Aurora* is operated by P&O Cruises and can carry 1,950 passengers and 850 crew. She had an extensive refit in 2007 after a whole series of unfortunate problems since she was launched in 2000; at the launch ceremony, performed by Princess Anne, the champagne bottle failed to break on the ship's hull a traditional sign of bad luck.

The 148,528 ton *Queen Mary II* in July 2004 paying her first visit to Scotland, photographed here in the Firth of Forth. The flagship of the Cunard fleet, she can accommodate 2,620 passengers and 1,253 crew and is now the only operational ocean liner in passenger service, although she also operates as a cruise ship.

At 154,407 tons the *Liberty of the Seas* is the world's largest cruise ship. Built in Finland to accommodate 4,370 passengers and 1,300 crew, she is seen here sailing up Southampton Water before docking at the port.

QUEEN ELIZABETH II

Known to everyone as the *QE2*, this Cunard liner was launched in 1967 and made her maiden voyage on 2nd May 1969. Built at a cost of £29 million by John Brown & Co Ltd on Clydebank, she was far from a giant, weighing 70,327 tons – considerably less than her namesake *Queen Elizabeth*. She could carry 2,283 passengers and a crew in excess of 1,000. Many innovations and much forward-thinking was applied to the design of the *QE2*. She had, for example, to pass through the Panama Canal, in order to fulfil the role of a cruise ship, which was essential with declining passenger demand for Atlantic crossings. She also used far less fuel than the old *Queens*. Cunard decided that maintaining a ship that was fast approaching 40 was too expensive a task and so she was sold to a Dubai investment group to be converted into a luxury hotel. Accordingly, the *QE2* arrived in Dubai on 26th November 2008. It was the end of an era.

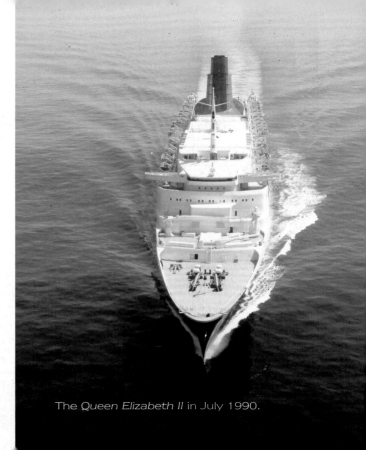

The *Queen Elizabeth II* in July 1990.

The *Queen Elizabeth II* in John Brown's yard, Clydebank in 1967.

The *Queen Elizabeth II* on sea trials off the Scottish coast in 1968.

The *Queen Elizabeth II* leaves New York Harbour, sailing past the Statue of Liberty in April 1992.

2008

The *Queen Elizabeth II* arrives at Southampton for the very last time before leaving to Dubai.

In November 2008 the *Queen Elizabeth II* visited Southampton before she sailed for Dubai to become a hotel.

Classic
AIRCRAFT

CIVIL AVIATION
from 1906 until
the present day

Available from all major stockists